The Constitution
and the
Bill of Rights

Roben Alarcon, M.A.Ed.

Table of Contents

Important Documents

The Constitution of the United States was written to explain how the country works. The government has three parts. Each part has a different job but the same amount of power. This protects the people in the country. People feel safe knowing that no part of the government can take over.

The Bill of Rights was added to the Constitution. These additions to the Constitution protect personal freedoms. Both **documents** were written more than 200 years ago and still make Americans free today.

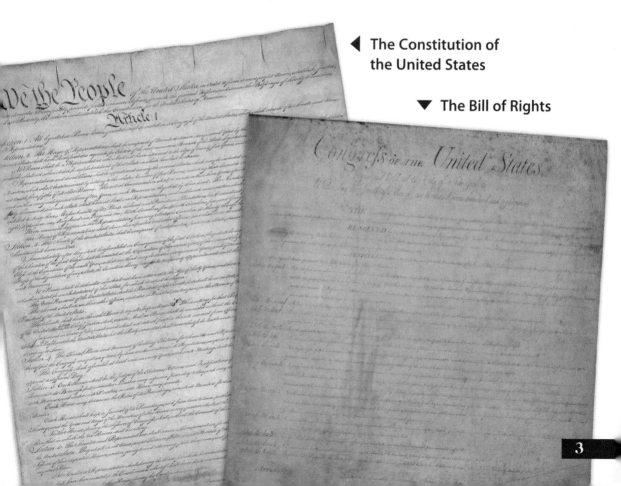

◀ The Constitution of the United States

▼ The Bill of Rights

A Better System

Every group of people needs organization so that work can get done. After the Revolutionary War, the **Continental** (kon-tuh-NEN-tuhl) **Congress** wrote America's first system of rules. These rules were called the Articles of Confederation (kuhn-fed-uh-RAY-shuhn). These rules did not give anyone enough power to do what needed to be done. The new country was in a lot of trouble.

Representatives (rep-ri-ZEN-tuh-tivs) from the different colonies held a meeting to rewrite the document. By the time they finished, they had made so many changes that it got a new name. It was called the Constitution of the United States of America.

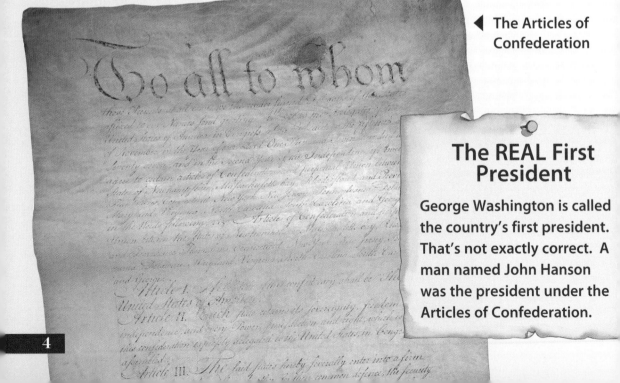

◀ The Articles of Confederation

The REAL First President

George Washington is called the country's first president. That's not exactly correct. A man named John Hanson was the president under the Articles of Confederation.

Some people complained about the **proposed** changes. Three important men decided to write letters to newspapers in New York. In the letters, they gave reasons why the new Constitution was a good form of government. Their letters, called "The Federalist Papers," made a difference. One by one, the states began to **ratify** the Constitution.

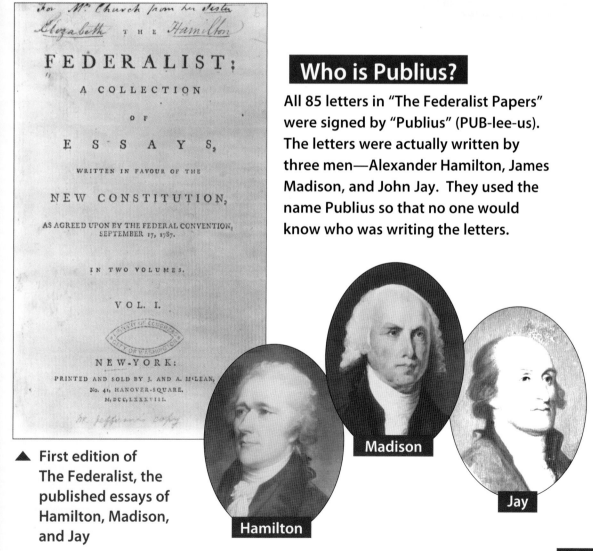

Who is Publius?

All 85 letters in "The Federalist Papers" were signed by "Publius" (PUB-lee-us). The letters were actually written by three men—Alexander Hamilton, James Madison, and John Jay. They used the name Publius so that no one would know who was writing the letters.

Madison

Jay

Hamilton

▲ First edition of The Federalist, the published essays of Hamilton, Madison, and Jay

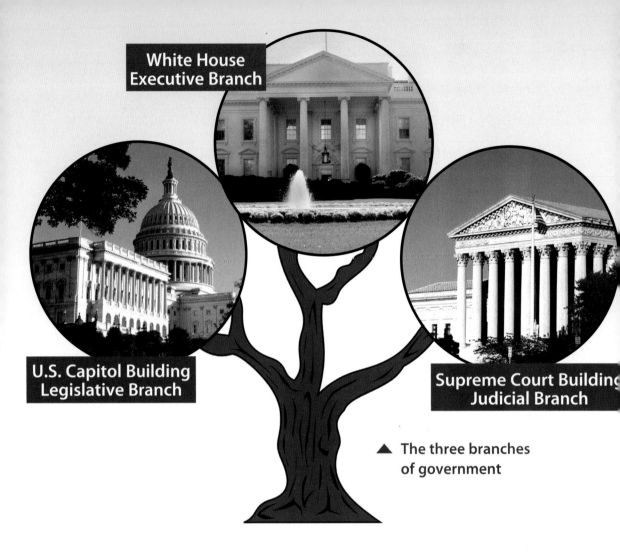

White House
Executive Branch

U.S. Capitol Building
Legislative Branch

Supreme Court Building
Judicial Branch

▲ The three branches
of government

Three Equal Parts

The writers of the Constitution thought the government should be divided into three parts: legislative (LEJ-is-lay-tiv), executive (eg-ZEK-yoo-tiv), and judicial (joo-DISH-uhl). The **legislative branch** makes new laws. The **executive branch** sees that the laws are followed. The **judicial branch** solves arguments about the laws. All three branches are needed for a good system.

The Weakest Branch?

Some people believed that the judicial branch was the weakest branch. This changed after the Marbury v. Madison Supreme Court case. The Supreme Court told the president that the executive branch had acted against the Constitution. It was the first time that the Supreme Court stood up to another branch of the government.

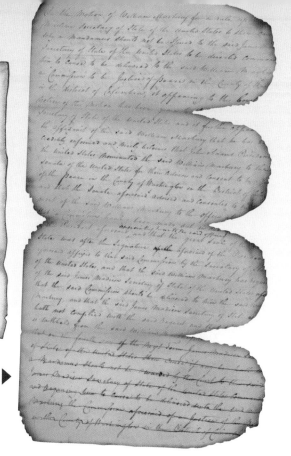

Supreme Court order ▶
given to Secretary of
State James Madison

The new Americans were afraid that one branch would become too strong. The king of Great Britain had used his power in a harmful way against them in the past. They never wanted that to happen again.

To make sure that no one person could get too much power, the writers of the Constitution created a system called "checks and balances." Each branch has its own job to do. At the same time, each branch has to watch over the other branches. For example, the president **nominates** the Supreme Court judges. The Senate then votes to say whether or not they agree with the choice. This is one way that the branches "check" each other.

We the People

The first 52 words in the Constitution are called the **Preamble** (PRE-am-buhl). These words explain why the Constitution was written. The Preamble begins with "We the people of the United States . . ."

Americans wanted a more "perfect union." That means that the states would have to act as a team so the country could be great. The Articles of Confederation did not help the states work together very well.

The colonists were angry about how King George III had treated them. They thought he was unfair. When they made the new government, the colonists wanted to "establish justice." This means to make sure the laws were fair for all people in America.

Popular Words

The words of the Preamble are very well known. You can buy T-shirts, posters, mugs, and all kinds of other fun items with "We the People" printed on them.

▼ The Preamble of the Constitution

Americans wanted "domestic tranquility" (duh-MES-tik trang-KWIL-eh-tee), which means peace in their new land. They thought the government should protect the people from harm by providing safety from all enemies.

The Preamble ends with, "And secure the Blessings of Liberty to ourselves and our **Posterity**" (po-STAIR-uh-tee). The Americans wrote the Constitution so they could be free forever.

▲ Signing the United States Constitution in 1787

The First State

Delaware was the first state to ratify the Constitution. The Delaware representative turned in the papers five days before the second state, Pennsylvania. Delaware is very proud of this achievement.

▲ The capitol building is home to the legislative branch.

Chosen to Make Laws

The legislative branch creates the country's laws. Two groups of people work together to do this. The House of Representatives and the Senate form **Congress**.

During the Constitutional Convention, people disagreed about how many representatives each state should have in Congress. Virginians thought that the larger states should have more people in Congress. Others thought that every state should have the same number of representatives. They did not think that **population** should matter. So, the two sides **compromised** and formed the House and the Senate.

Each state has two senators. Therefore, every state is equally represented as laws are created in the Senate.

In the House of Representatives, the number of representatives from each state depends on how many people live there. Larger states have more members in the House.

How Long?

Strom Thurmond served in the U.S. Senate longer than anyone else did. He was a senator for 47 years!

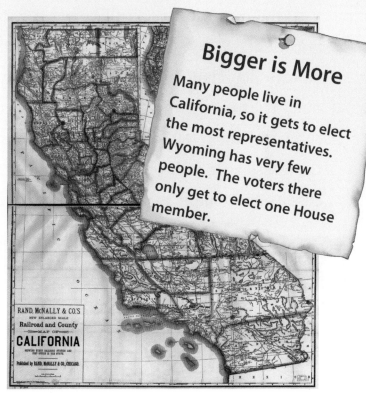

Bigger is More

Many people live in California, so it gets to elect the most representatives. Wyoming has very few people. The voters there only get to elect one House member.

▲ Map of California, the state with the highest population

Biggest Library in the World

You better really like to read if you visit the Library of Congress. It has about 530 miles (853 km) of bookshelves.

◀ Interior of the Library of Congress building in Washington, D.C.

Extra Duties

The people in Congress don't just create laws. They have other responsibilities, too. They make changes to the nation's money. They also make decisions about the military.

One important job of Congress is "checking" on the president. When Congress passes a bill, the president can say no, or **veto**, it. That does not automatically mean the bill is thrown out. There is one more chance for every vetoed bill. Congress can **override** a veto. The bill becomes a law if two-thirds of Congress vote in favor of the bill again. This is one way that checks and balances work.

▲ This shows the Senate during the impeachment trial of Andrew Johnson.

Andrew Johnson

Congress can also **impeach** a president. If Congress thinks a president has done something very wrong, they can hold a trial. Senators decide if the president is guilty or not. If they think he is guilty, he is no longer allowed to be president.

Richard Nixon

War Powers Act

In 1973, Congress wanted a new law called the War Powers Act. This law would force the president to talk to Congress before sending Americans to war. President Richard Nixon vetoed the bill. He thought the president should be allowed to decide these things alone. Congress voted to override his veto and it became a law.

Impeaching the Presidents

Only two presidents have been impeached, Andrew Johnson and Bill Clinton. Both were judged by the Senate and found not guilty. President Richard Nixon thought he was going to be impeached. He resigned and did not have to go to trial.

Bill Clinton

▲ President Washington and his cabinet

Commander in Chief

The executive branch makes sure the laws are followed, or enforces the laws. The president is the head of this branch. He has a group of people called the **cabinet** to help him.

The vice president is one of the cabinet members. He must be ready to take over if anything happens to the president.

Each of the cabinet members has an important job. One person watches the education system. Another person keeps an eye on farms and crops. A third is in charge of the protection of the country. There are many people in the cabinet to let the president know what is happening in the country.

The Constitution has special rules about who can become president. The **candidate** must be 35 years or older and born in the United States. He or she also must have lived in the country for 14 years. It hasn't happened yet, but a woman can be president, too.

An American in Death

President Andrew Johnson's body was wrapped in the American flag when he was buried. A copy of the Constitution was the pillow under his head.

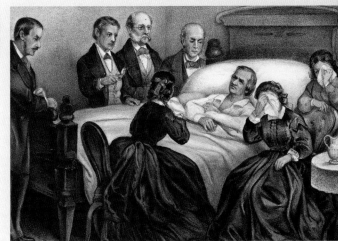

▲ Andrew Johnson on his deathbed

Roosevelt Vetoes

Franklin D. Roosevelt vetoed more bills than any other president did—635 in all! On the other hand, Thomas Jefferson never vetoed any bills while he was president.

Franklin D. Roosevelt

The National Court System

The judicial branch is made up of all the courts in the country. The courts have the important job of **interpreting** laws. They decide what laws really mean and how they should be used. The courts can also decide if Congress has passed a law that goes against the Constitution. When that happens, the law is removed and no longer used.

▲ U.S. Supreme Court building in Washington, D.C.

Salmon P. Chase

Money Judge

One Supreme Court judge, Salmon P. Chase, actually had his face on money! He is the only judge to ever be shown on a bill. He was on the $10,000 bill, which is no longer made.

Federal judges are chosen by the president. Then the Senate has to approve the person for the job. Once a federal judge has a job, he or she can keep it for life. The only way a judge can be fired is by impeachment. This means the president and the Senate have to be very careful about whom they choose.

▼ This is the Senate journal describing the Pickering trial.

First Judge Impeached

Just like a president, a judge can be impeached. The first judge to be impeached was John Pickering in 1804. He was forced to give up his job. Some people think he was impeached because he had strange ideas of how the government should be. Others think it was just because he was a rude man.

THE TRIAL OF JOHN PICKERING,

JUDGE OF THE NEW HAMPSHIRE DISTRICT,

ON A CHARGE EXHIBITED TO

THE SENATE OF THE UNITED STATES,

FOR HIGH CRIMES AND MISDEMEANORS.

IN SENATE OF THE UNITED STATES,

THURSDAY, MARCH 3, 1803.

A message was received from the House of Representatives, by Messrs. Nicholson and Randolph, two of the members of said House, in the words following:

Mr. President: We are commanded, in the name of the House of Repre nd of all the people of the United States, to impeach John Pickering, ju district court of the district of New Hampshire, of high crimes and misdemeanors, and to acquaint the Senate that the House of Representatives will, in due time, exhibit par ticular articles of impeachment against him, and make good the same.

We are further commanded to demand that the S

▲ The nine justices of the Supreme Court in 1888

The Supreme Court

The highest court in the United States is the Supreme Court. There are always nine **justices**, or judges, on the Supreme Court. The chief justice is the judge who is in charge. Being chosen as a judge for the Supreme Court is a great honor.

Sometimes, this court hears new cases, but usually the cases have already been through other courts. When a person

Sandra Day O'Connor

Sandra Day O'Connor was the first woman to serve as a United States Supreme Court justice.

▼ John Jay, the first Supreme Court chief justice

Red Robes?

The first Supreme Court judges wore red and black robes. In 1800, justices began to wear the black robes they wear today.

loses a court case, he or she usually thinks it's not fair. So, the person tries to get a higher court to listen to the case. This can happen over and over. The case might move through many levels of the court system. Finally, special cases make it all the way to the Supreme Court. The Supreme Court's decision is final.

Changing the Constitution

When the Constitution was being written, many **delegates** were worried. They wanted to make sure the government didn't have too much power. They kept thinking about Great Britain's power over them when they were colonists.

Some of the delegates were upset by the final document. The rights of the people were not included. This meant that the federal government could abuse its power.

James Madison

▲ The Constitutional Conventi◀

◀ Madison was called the "Father of the Constitution" because he took very careful notes during the Constitutional Convention.

George Mason

George Mason was very excited about the Constitution at first. He got upset when he found out there would be no list of rights for the people. He said he "would sooner chop off his right hand" than sign the Constitution without listing personal rights.

George Mason of Virginia said, "It has no declaration of rights!" Mason had written a bill of rights in the Virginia State Constitution. He really wanted one to be included in the United States Constitution as well.

By 1791, the Bill of Rights was added. The Bill of Rights is the first ten **amendments**, or changes, to the Constitution.

Changing the Document

Over the past 200 years, only 17 other amendments have been added to the Constitution.

The First Amendment protects the right of Freedom of Assembly. This allows people to have marches such as the March on Washington in 1963.

The Rights of All People

The Bill of Rights got its name because these first ten amendments protect the rights of all Americans. These amendments and others help people to know that the government cannot hurt them.

Many people think the First Amendment is the most important. It protects people in many ways. Americans can follow any religion they want. Americans can say what they want without having to be afraid. Newspaper and magazines can decide what stories to print. People can meet together and talk about the country's problems. The government is not allowed to stop any of this.

The Fifth Amendment protects people who have been arrested. Each accused person gets to have a court case before being called guilty. Also, no one is forced to speak in his or her own trial.

The United States Constitution and the Bill of Rights are powerful documents. Each protects Americans in its own way. The Constitution makes sure that no part of government has too much power. The Bill of Rights gives personal rights to all people. Both show how important freedom is to all Americans.

Pleading the Fifth

The Fifth Amendment protects people when they testify in court. When a lawyer asks a question, the person on the stand can "plead the fifth." This means the person is allowed to stay quiet and not answer any questions. This is one way that people can protect themselves during a trial.

▼ Defendants have the right to a trial by jury because of the Sixth Amendment.

Rough Discipline

In 1977, two students sued their junior high school. They said that the principal was using "cruel and unusual punishment." Both boys had been paddled very harshly. They even had to see a doctor. The students felt this abused their rights under the Eighth Amendment. The Supreme Court did not agree. The Court said that the Eighth Amendment did not have anything to do with school discipline. It was written to protect people who had been arrested.

Glossary

amendments—changes made to the Constitution; two-thirds of the states must agree

cabinet—people who advise the president on how to run the country

candidate— person who is running for office

compromised—settled the problem by each group giving up something

Congress—main group of lawmakers for the United States government; made of two groups—the House of Representatives and the Senate

Continental Congress—meeting of the lawmakers for the original 13 colonies

delegates—people sent to speak for the group

documents—official papers

executive branch—part of the government that must carry out the laws

federal—relating to the main government of the United States

impeach—accuse a public official of doing wrong and taking the official to court

interpreting—figuring out the meaning

judicial branch—part of the government that must decide what the laws mean

justices—judges in a court

legislative branch—part of the government that makes the laws

nominates—suggests someone for a position

override—to cancel a decision

population—total number of people who live in an area

posterity— future generations of people

preamble—an introduction

proposed—suggested

ratify—to officially agree or approve

representatives—people sent to speak for a group; also the name given to people who work in the House of Representatives

veto—how a president stops a bill from becoming a law